A Taste of culture

Foods of India

Barbara Sheen

KIDHAVEN PRESS
An imprint of Thomson Gale, a part of The Thomson Corporation

THOMSON
━━━━━✦━━━━━ ™
GALE

Detroit • New York • San Francisco • New Haven, Conn. • Waterville, Maine • London

LIBRARY OF CONGRESS CATALOGING-IN-PUBLICATION DATA

Sheen, Barbara.
   Foods of India / by Barbara Sheen.
     p. cm. — (A taste of culture)
Includes bibliographical references and index.
ISBN-13: 978-0-7377-3553-6 (hardcover : alk. paper)
ISBN-10: 0-7377-3553-8 (hardcover : alk. paper)
1. Cookery, Indic—Juvenile literature. 2. India—Social life and customs—Juvenile literature. I. Title.
TX724.5.I4S445 2007
641.5954—dc22

              2006018758

Printed in the United States of America

Contents

Colorful, Fragrant, and Delicious

Indian cooking is colorful, fragrant, and delicious. It depends on a wide array of spices, legumes, and grains for its distinct character.

An Ancient Treasure

India is the world's chief supplier of spices and has been for at least thirty-six hundred years. These fragrant and flavorful plant substances, which often have been more prized than jewels, have drawn people from all over the world to India throughout history.

Unlike spice seekers from other nations, Indians have always had access to a wide array of different spices. Some of the most popular spices include mint, bright orange turmeric, pungent cumin, sweet and refreshing

Distribution of Foods and Spices

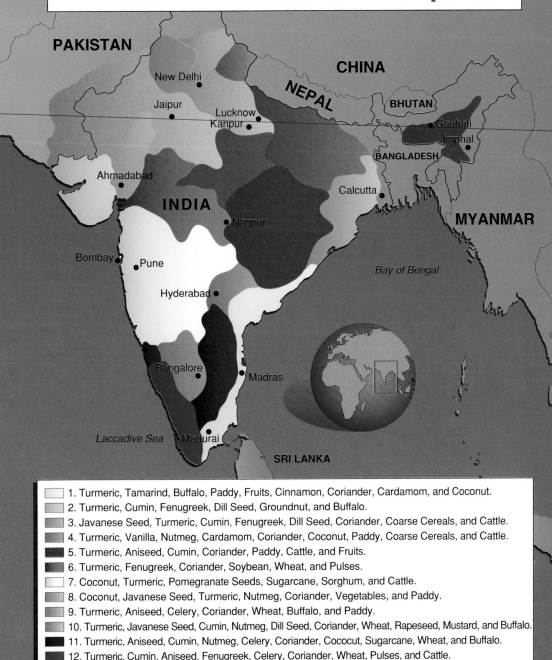

1. Turmeric, Tamarind, Buffalo, Paddy, Fruits, Cinnamon, Coriander, Cardamom, and Coconut.
2. Turmeric, Cumin, Fenugreek, Dill Seed, Groundnut, and Buffalo.
3. Javanese Seed, Turmeric, Cumin, Fenugreek, Dill Seed, Coriander, Coarse Cereals, and Cattle.
4. Turmeric, Vanilla, Nutmeg, Cardamom, Coriander, Coconut, Paddy, Coarse Cereals, and Cattle.
5. Turmeric, Aniseed, Cumin, Coriander, Paddy, Cattle, and Fruits.
6. Turmeric, Fenugreek, Coriander, Soybean, Wheat, and Pulses.
7. Coconut, Turmeric, Pomegranate Seeds, Sugarcane, Sorghum, and Cattle.
8. Coconut, Javanese Seed, Turmeric, Nutmeg, Coriander, Vegetables, and Paddy.
9. Turmeric, Aniseed, Celery, Coriander, Wheat, Buffalo, and Paddy.
10. Turmeric, Javanese Seed, Cumin, Nutmeg, Dill Seed, Coriander, Wheat, Rapeseed, Mustard, and Buffalo.
11. Turmeric, Aniseed, Cumin, Nutmeg, Celery, Coriander, Cococut, Sugarcane, Wheat, and Buffalo.
12. Turmeric, Cumin, Aniseed, Fenugreek, Celery, Coriander, Wheat, Pulses, and Cattle.
13. Turmeric, Aniseed, Cumin, Fenugreek, Coriander, Celery, Buffalo, Cattle, and Wheat.
14. Coriander, Celery, Turmeric, Javanese Seed, Aniseed, Fenugreek, Paddy, Wheat, and Cattle.
15. Tamarind, Coriander, Coconut, Turmeric, Groundnut, Paddy, and Fruits.

Many different ingredients make up an Indian masala, or spice mixture.

cardamom, parsley-like coriander, bitter-tasting **kari** (cah-ree), cinnamon, and mustard seeds. Indian chefs have been using these and other delicious spices to preserve, color, flavor, and perfume their food for thousands of years. Indian cuisine would not be the same without them.

An Artful Combination

Indians use spices the way artists use paint, blending them together in hundreds of different combinations and proportions. For a dish to be considered well cooked, no single spice should ever dominate. Instead there must be a perfect balance of ingredients, with each dish having its own distinctive taste, color, and perfume. This means that cooks need to understand the characteristics of each spice and how they mix together. Chef Mridula Baljekar explains: "Spices are the heart and soul of Indian cooking. Knowing how to use the spices is the key that unlocks the secrets of alluring aromas and magical flavors of classic Indian cuisine."[1]

Indian cooks blend spices in a number of ways. They create a **masala** (mah-saah-laah), a general term that refers to any combination of ground spices. They make masala by grinding different spices together into a powder. This may be done in a stone dish known as a mortar with a small, wooden, clublike tool called a pestle. A food processor can also be used to save time. **Garam masala** (gah-rahm mah-saah-laah), a favorite spice mixture, is a specific blend of up to fifteen spices that is widely used in Indian cooking. It features cinnamon, black pepper, cloves, cardamom, and other spices. It is dark and zesty.

Spices are also used whole. Roots, pods, seeds, and leaves are fried for less than a minute in hot oil or **ghee** (gee). Ghee is a type of butter in which all the milk solids have been removed. Incredibly fragrant, the spiced or tempered oil is used as a basis for hundreds of different sauces.

Rice and Grains

Sauces are often served over rice, a staple of the Indian diet and an important part of Indian culture. Rice symbolizes good fortune in India, which is why rice porridge is the first solid food fed to babies. It is also the most important crop in India, with one-fourth of all cultivated land planted with it.

Although many varieties of rice are grown, basmati (bas-maah-tee) rice is the most popular. It is known for its smooth, rich taste and fresh aroma. *Basmati* literally means "the queen of perfumes" in Hindi, one of the most common languages spoken in India. Indians have many uses for basmati rice. It is boiled and topped with a spicy sauce filled with meat or vegetables. It can also be stir-fried with spices, used in puddings, puffed into a popcorn-like snack, or cooked in aromatic casseroles.

Indians eat about 4½ pounds (2 kg) of rice a week. Before cooking it, they carefully rinse the rice. This removes impurities and excess starch and keeps the grains from sticking together. Then the rice is soaked for at least an hour before it is boiled. Soaking whitens the

Rice with Cumin

This is a wonderfully scented rice dish. It uses basmati rice, but any long-grain rice can be substituted. Cumin seeds are sold in the spice section of supermarkets.

Ingredients
1 tablespoon vegetable oil for frying
1 teaspoon cumin seeds
½ teaspoon black pepper
2 cups basmati or other long grain rice
4 cups water
½ teaspoon salt

Instructions
1. Heat the oil in a large saucepan over medium heat. Add the cumin and pepper. Stir-fry for about 45 seconds. Add the rice and stir-fry for one minute.
2. Add the water and salt. Bring the rice to a boil. Reduce heat to low, cover the pan, and simmer until the water is absorbed and the rice is tender, about ten minutes.
3. Remove the rice from heat. Leave the rice covered for about five minutes. Uncover carefully, because hot steam will escape. Fluff with a fork and serve.

Serves 4.

A rice vendor sells packets of Basmati rice.

Indian flat breads called rotis cook on a hot griddle outdoors.

rice and helps the grains absorb the flavor of the spicy sauces that will be poured over them. According to authors Martin Hughes, Sheema Mookherjee, and Richard Delacy, the end result is, "white, long, and silky."[2]

Wonderful Breads

Although rice is eaten at every meal in southern India and in great quantities in northern India, flat breads known as **rotis** (ro-tees) are the core of northern meals. Rotis are also popular in the rest of the nation. Roti originated centuries ago as a portable food that farmers and shepherds could dine on when they were out in the fields. Today Indians use rotis like edible spoons to scoop up saucy dishes, meat, and vegetables.

Rotis are made without yeast from nutrient-rich whole-wheat flour, which is mixed with water and kneaded to form a thin dough. The dough is divided into tennis ball–size portions, rolled into almost perfect circles, and cooked on a hot cast-iron griddle known as a **tawa** (tah-waah).

Cooks make a wide variety of rotis, but the most common is **chapati** (chah-paah-tee), a soft flat bread that balloons out as it cooks. Other favorites include **pooris** (poo-rees), which are deep-fried chapatis, and **paranthas** (pah-rahn-thahs), which have a pastry-like texture. Many Indian cooks make fresh roti for every meal. Traditionally the woman of the house makes the bread as the family eats. When the roti is done, she brushes it with butter to keep it soft and transfers it from the griddle to the table. "This is simple . . . home cooking," explains a chef at the Indian Foods Company. "I cannot go for many days without my roti."[3]

Colorful Legumes

Legumes are another essential part of the Indian diet. Legumes such as lentils, beans, and peas are eaten at least once a day. They are usually flavored and scented with spices and served over rice, or with roti and a vegetable. Since they are loaded with vitamins, minerals, protein and fiber they are quite nutritious. This may be

Lentil Dal

This simple dal recipe uses lentils. Yellow split peas can be substituted.

Ingredients
1 cup dried lentils
2 cups water
½ teaspoon salt
½ teaspoon turmeric
½ teaspoon cayenne pepper
1 onion, finely chopped
1 tablespoon minced garlic
1 tablespoon vegetable oil or butter for frying

Instructions
1. Combine lentils, water, salt, and turmeric in a saucepan and bring to a boil. Lower the heat, cover the pan, and simmer until the lentils are cooked and much of the water is absorbed, about twenty minutes. The mixture should be soft and thick when done. If the mixture starts to stick to the pot during cooking, add more water.
2. Heat oil in a frying pan. Add onions, garlic, and cayenne pepper. Fry over low heat until the onions are translucent.
3. Stir the onion mixture into the lentils. Serve with rice.

Serves 4.

Vegetables

Indians eat a lot of vegetables. Vegetables are served at almost every meal and are cooked in a wide variety of ways. They are often the main ingredients in spicy sauce dishes. They are roasted in a tandoor, made into fritters, threaded on kabobs, stir-fried, or mashed.

Some Indian vegetables are familiar to Westerners, while others are not. Potatoes, onions, spinach, eggplant, cabbage, cauliflower, and thin, sweet carrots are very popular. White pumpkins, which are cooked in a spicy sauce, are less familiar. Other unusual vegetables include purple and white yams, various edible gourds, the roots of the lotus flower, and white radishes. Plantains, large, green, banana-like fruits, are fried and sprinkled with spices.

why an Indian proverb says that legumes and roti are all an Indian needs to survive. Indian cooks use over 60 different types of legumes. These include tiny yellow split peas; black, yellow, and pink lentils; and tan chickpeas. One of the favorite ways of using legumes is in **dal** (dahl), a delicious stewlike dish. Each cook has his or her own dal recipes, so there are countless variations. Depending on the cook, dal can contain just one type of legume or a few. It can be thick and chunky, or the lentils may be mashed so that the dal is thin and velvety smooth. But what gives dal its special taste and aroma are the spices that flavor it.

To make dal, cooks soak the legumes overnight to soften them. Then they simmer them for hours. When

A vendor displays her wares at an outdoor fruit and vegetable market in Pushkar, India.

the legumes are tender, selected spices are cooked in hot oil or ghee and added to the legumes right before they are served. This gives the legumes, which are otherwise bland, a savory flavor and a mouthwatering aroma. Popular combinations include pink lentils spiced with cumin, pepper, and chili powder, or yellow split peas flavored with mashed garlic, ginger, and cinnamon.

Pea Pod

Mint is often added to the stew. And sometimes yogurt is mixed into dal to give it a creamy texture. One thing is certain: No matter the ingredients, Indians love dal. "There is something wonderfully warm and tasty about . . . dal," explains chef Suvir Saran. "I want [it] when I have a craving for something simple and homey, but still savory."[4]

Indian cooking is, indeed, warm and tasty. Indian chefs artfully combine brightly colored legumes, richly perfumed spices, and deliciously satisfying grains to create dishes that are uniquely Indian.

Common Threads

India is a large country with many geographic differences. Plains, deserts, thousands of miles of coastline dotted with tropical beaches, and snow-capped mountains all are a part of India. This geographic diversity affects what the 1 billion people who live here eat. For example, coconuts, seafood, and tropical fruit are popular on the coasts where they are cultivated. Thick stews that warm the body are favorites in the cold mountains.

Religious rules also influence the Indian diet. Indians are divided into a number of religious groups. Eighty percent are Hindus and 13 percent are Muslims. There are also Sikhs and Buddhists, among others. Few Muslims eat pork, while most Hindus avoid beef. Many Hindus, Sikhs, and Buddhists are vegetarians. As a matter of fact, there are more vegetarians in India than in any other nation. Despite these differences, the use of spices and similar cooking methods bind all Indian cooking together.

Spicy Sauces

Curry is probably the most famous of all Indian foods. It is not a single dish and there is no basic recipe for it. Curry actually describes any dish cooked in a spicy

Mealtime is a special time for this boy and his family.

Spicy chicken curry is just one of many curries enjoyed by Indians.

sauce. This usage dates from the mid-1800s when the British ruled India. The British used the word *curry*, taken from the spicy Indian herb kari, for all spicy dishes. A wide range of popular, stewlike dishes are bathed in zesty sauces. Each has different main ingredients, but the basis for every one is a savory sauce made from a blend of aromatic spices.

Indian cooks create these sauces in layers. First a combination of spices, which usually includes garam masala, is cooked in hot oil or ghee with nuts or grated onions.

Then yogurt, which adds a pleasant tartness, or tomatoes follow. The main ingredients, which include a variety of vegetables and/or meat or seafood, come next. Water is added, and the stew is cooked until all the flavors blend deliciously and the ingredients are buttery soft.

Eating in India

Some mealtime customs in India are different from customs in North America. For instance, in India food is rarely served in serving bowls. Instead, each diner is given a round metal tray called a *thali* (taah-lee). On it are small bowls containing different dishes such as rice, dal, chicken korma, potatoes, chutney, and raita.

Instead of utensils, food is eaten with the right hand. The left hand, which is used for personal hygiene, is never used for eating. Diners use the tips of their fingers to pick up food and their thumbs to scoop the food into their mouths.

A thali, or food tray, holds a variety of foods and seasonings.

A favorite Indian dinner includes the hot and spicy stew called roghan josh, dal, rice, and flat breads.

Many Dishes

Indians make hundreds of different kinds of saucy, stew-like dishes, which are eaten with rice or roti. Depending on the spices, the stews can be fiery or mild. **Kormas** (kor-maahs), for instance, are rich and mild. Main ingredients such as vegetables, chicken, lamb, or seafood are smothered in a creamy sauce flavored with cinnamon, nutmeg, pepper, and mustard seeds. The mixture is then thickened with coconut milk and almond paste. The result is fragrant, velvety, and delicious.

Zestier stews are also quite popular. **Roghan josh** (ro-gahn josh) is hot and spicy. Its sauce is made with garam masala cooked with lamb and topped with fried tomatoes and onions. **Vindaloo** (vin-dah-loo) dishes are even hotter. Pork vindaloo is popular, but vindaloos also feature vegetables or lamb. The main ingredient is marinated in a sweet-and-sour sauce made of vinegar, ginger, and garlic. This mixture is then topped with a second sauce flavored with cumin, turmeric, and whole, dried chilis. Even though vindaloo dishes are fiery, the taste is not unpleasant. Like all Indian stews, vindaloo has a delicate flavor that lingers on the palate. "I call this back heat," explains Suvir Saran. "It goes and goes in your mouth long after you've swallowed the bite!"[5]

Crisp, Moist, and Succulent

Other deliciously spiced foods are cooked in a **tandoor** (tahn-dur). A tandoor is a barrel-shaped clay oven. It was brought to India in the 10th century by Persians fleeing their Arab conquerers.

Much like Americans have barbeque grills, some Indians have a tandoor in their backyards. For those who do not have one, there are tandoor restaurants, which are the most popular restaurants in India.

To use a tandoor, cooks build a charcoal fire in its bottom. The heat can reach as high as 850°F (450°C). Such intense heat cooks food rapidly and locks in moisture. Food cooked in a tandoor is crisp on the outside and soft and juicy within.

Flat breads are baked over high heat in a tandoor.

Most any food can be cooked in a tandoor. And many different foods can be grilled, baked, or roasted at the same time. "It must be the most versatile oven in the world," says Baljekar. "The cook can, as if by waving a magic wand, produce a variety of dishes."[6]

Chicken Tikka

Chicken tikka can be made on a grill or in an oven. The longer the chicken marinates, the tastier it gets.

Ingredients
½ cup plain yogurt
juice of 1 lemon
1 teaspoon cayenne pepper
1 teaspoon chili powder
1 teaspoon grated ginger
1 teaspoon turmeric
1 teaspoon salt
1 tablespoon tomato sauce
4 chicken breasts, cut into cubes

Instructions
1. Mix all the ingredients except the chicken together in a large bowl. Add the chicken. Put in the refrigerator to marinate one hour to overnight.
2. Preheat the oven to 375°F. Put the chicken on skewers. Place the skewers across a drip tray sprayed with nonstick spray or lined with aluminum foil.
3. Cook the meat until it is no longer pink inside, about twenty minutes. Serve with mint chutney.

Serves 4.

Mint Chutney

Mint chutney is served with almost every meal. Chopped green mango can be used to add tartness. Use more chilis for a spicier taste and fewer for a milder taste.

Ingredients
1 cup fresh mint leaves
1 cup fresh cilantro, chopped
3 green onions, chopped
2 green chilis, chopped, seeds and stem removed
1 teaspoon minced ginger
1 teaspoon minced garlic
1 teaspoon sugar
½ teaspoon salt
2 tablespoons water
juice of one lemon

Instructions
1. Combine all ingredients in a food processor or blender. Puree until the mixture becomes a paste.
2. Makes one cup. Refrigerate until ready to serve. Serve with any Indian dish or with crackers.

Until the 19th century, tandoors were used just to bake **naan** (nahn), an Indian flat bread. Naan is made by pressing dough onto the hot oven's walls. Many Indian villages had a communal tandoor in the middle of the town that villagers used to make their bread.

Today whole chickens, known as tandoori chicken, and chunks of lamb or chicken, known as tikka (tee-kah) kebabs, are commonly made in the clay oven. To make these dishes, the cook marinates the meat in a spice-laden yogurt mixture. The marinade flavors and tenderizes the meat. The spice mix, called tandoori masala, includes flavorless red food coloring that gives the food a vivid,reddish-pink hue.

Because the longer meat marinates, the more intense the flavor, this step can range from an hour to days. Before it is placed in the oven, the meat is brushed with ghee. Then it is threaded through a long, metal skewer and cooked. The cooked meat or chicken is served with rice or roti, cooked onions, and various relishes. It is incredibly succulent and smells delicious. "The food absorbs both the subtle earthy scent naturally released by the clay and the wisps of fragrant smoke created by . . . drops of marinade falling on the white-hot coals,"[7] explains an expert at Golden Tandoors, a company that designs ovens.

Flavorful Accompaniments

Whether Indians are feasting on tandoori chicken or roghan josh, no meal is considered complete without **raitas** (rye-tahs) and **chutneys**. Served in small, round bowls and eaten right along with the rest of the meal, these lightly spiced relishes cool the palate and bring still more flavor and color to the table. Cooks mix together yogurt, raw vegetables or fruits, and various spices to make cool and creamy raitas. The relishes provide a soothing contrast to highly spiced dishes.

There are hundreds of different kinds of raitas. Cucumber-mint raita is one of the most popular. Pineapple

A vendor's boat is filled with a variety of vegetables for market.

raita, which blends the sweet fruit with yogurt and a bit of pepper, is a delightful mix of different flavors.

Chutneys also come in a wide range of flavors. These homemade, fresh relishes contain fruits and vegetables cut into tiny pieces and delicately flavored with spices. Chef Diane Seed explains: "Most Indian families take pride in their homemade . . . chutneys. . . . Houses are adorned with rows of jars maturing in the sun on the windowsills, and a hostess is often judged by the number of relishes she serves."[8]

It is quite common for a variety of raitas and chutneys to be served at one time, and each cook has his or her own special recipes. Mint chutney, which combines fresh mint, onions, garlic, and lemon juice, is quite popular. Coconut chutney is also a favorite. It mixes freshly grated coconut with ginger, garlic, kari leaves, and dried chilis. Other chutneys are made from tomatoes, green mangoes, and apples. All are brightly colored and taste sweet, hot, and tart all at the same time.

No matter where you go in India, chutney and raita are likely to be served. Although Indian cooking is diverse, flavorful dishes cooked in spicy sauces or in a tandoor oven and served with these tasty relishes are loved throughout India. Such dishes share similar cooking methods and a common use of spices. These are the threads that tie all Indian cooking together.

Chapter 3

Tasty Snacks

Indians love to snack. Street stalls and roving food vendors can be found in every city and village. "Whatever the time of day, people are boiling, frying, roasting, peeling, juicing, simmering, mixing, or baking some class of food and drink to lure passers-by," explain Hughes, Mookherjee, and Delacy. "Snacking is second nature to Indians. . . . They don't snack to tide them over between meals, they snack because they love the food."[9] Among the most popular snacks are savory fried treats and deliciously spiced tea.

Made-to-Order Treats

Indians enjoy a wide variety of fragrant, deep-fried snacks called **chaats** (chahts). These are flavored with chaat masala, a blend of sea salt, cumin, dried mango powder, chili powder, and ginger, and served with chutney. Among the most popular are samosas (sah-mo-saahs), panipuris (pahn-nee poo-rees), pakoras (pah-kaw-raahs), and pakodas (pah-koo-dahs).

Samosas are small, triangular pastries. They are filled with vegetables seasoned with chaat masala. Mashed potatoes and peas are one of the most popular

A Mumbai street vendor prepares pao-bhaji, Indian fast food, for hungry on-the-go customers.

Piping hot samosas have been a favorite Indian snack for centuries.

fillings. Indians have been snacking on samosas since ancient Persian spice traders brought them to India. The traders made the crispy, portable treats on their campfires at night, then packed them for the next day's journey. Samosas quickly became popular in India and by the 14th century were a favorite snack of almost everyone, including Indian royalty.

Panipuris are also filled pastries. These bite-size treats are made of puffed fried bread that is lightly crushed open on one side. This forms a small, shell-like container that holds the filling. Popular fillings include chickpeas or mashed potatoes topped with onions and chutney.

Vegetable Pakodas

This recipe uses an onion, eggplant, and bell pepper, but almost any vegetable can be used. Indians use chickpea flour, but any flour will work.

Ingredients
2 cups flour
1 cup water
½ teaspoon baking soda
1 teaspoon cayenne pepper
1 teaspoon salt
½ cup vegetable oil for frying
1 small bell pepper, cut into thin rounds
1 small onion, cut into thin rounds
1 small eggplant, cut into thin rounds

Instructions
1. Combine all the ingredients except the vegetables and oil to make a thin batter.
2. Heat the oil in a deep frying pan.
3. Dip the vegetable slices in the batter and fry a few at a time. Be sure to fry both sides. Remove the vegetables from the pan when they are golden brown. Drain on a paper towel. Serve hot with chutney.

Serves 4 to 8.

Snackers typically pop the whole thing into their mouths. Just one bite releases an explosion of different flavors. It is no wonder that it is almost impossible to eat just one. But since a half dozen generally costs less than 50 cents, thrifty snackers can easily indulge their appetites.

Pakoras and pakodas are two other fried treats. Pakoras are vegetable fritters or patties. They are made

Pakoras, fritters made from ground vegetables, are often served with a variety of chutneys.

with ground vegetables, chaat masala, and chickpea flour. They are fried in hot oil or ghee until they are crisp and golden. Potato, eggplant, zucchini, and cauliflower are all popular ingredients for pakoras.

Pakodas are similar to pakoras. But instead of ground vegetables formed into little fritters, pakodas are more like fried onion rings. They are made by deep-frying vegetable rings breaded with spiced flour. Almost any vegetable is used. Cauliflower, eggplant, spinach, and mushrooms all make delicious pakodas.

All chaats are made-to-order. Snackers choose their favorite fillings, or breaded vegetable, and hot or sweet chutney. Before the chaat is served, chaat masala is sprinkled over it. How much depends on the individual. With so many choices, it is not surprising that every chaat is slightly different. But one thing is the same: They never taste greasy. That is because the cook closely monitors the cooking temperature. If it is too hot, the oil will smoke. The chaat will burn on the outside but be soggy and undercooked within. If it is too cool, the chaat will absorb the cooking oil and taste greasy. But when the temperature is just right, chaats are so light and flaky that they melt in the mouth. "I don't know anyone who doesn't enjoy these wonderfully crisp finger foods,"[10] says Baljekar.

Healthy Fast Food

Pav bhaji (pahv bhah-jee), a juicy bread-and-vegetable mixture, is as popular in India as hamburgers are in America. It originated as a cheap late-night snack for hungry mill workers in the city of Bombay (now Mumbai) but quickly became popular with other Indians.

Pav is a square bread, similar to a dinner roll. Bhaji is a mix of vegetables and spices. The vegetables and spices almost always feature potatoes and may also include peas, onions, cauliflower, and tomatoes. These ingredients are mashed together on a hot griddle and cooked until hot and tender. At the same time, the bread is cut open, slathered with butter, sprinkled with masala, and roasted on the griddle until the butter melts and the bread is golden. The vegetables and bread are served beside each other on a flat dish with chopped onions and various chutneys.

A cook stirs a large pot of mashed vegetables to be used to make pav bhaji, a popular Indian fast-food dish.

Pav bhaji is one of the most popular snacks in India. Although it is considered a fast food, the vegetables make it quite nutritious. Explains Gel, an Indian mother, "This Mumbai street food is my family's all time favorite food. It is similar to the Sloppy Joe, of the West. What's so great about this wonderful dish is that it is packed with the goodness of many vegetables. How many junk food recipes can boast that?"[11]

Fragrant Tea

When thirsty Indians want a beverage to go with a savory snack, they often choose **chai** (cha-ee). Chai is a sweet,

Lassi

Lassi (lah-see) is a yogurt-based drink similar to a smoothie or milkshake. It is popular throughout India. Lassis can be sweet or salty. Sweet lassis are usually made with fresh fruit such as mangoes. The fruit is mixed with yogurt, ice, cold water, and sugar. Spices such as cardamom and black pepper may also be added. Salty lassis include mint, salt, and cumin with the yogurt mix. Some lassis substitute ground nuts, such as pistachios, instead of fruit or mint. Lassis are served cold and are quite refreshing.

Frothy lassi is a refreshing yogurt-based drink.

An Indian holy man enjoys a glass of chai while viewing the sights of Mumbai.

milky, spiced tea. India is the world's largest producer and consumer of tea. Most Indians drink the hot liquid at least twice a day. They enjoy it in the morning with biscuits for dunking and once again with a spicy snack at teatime in the afternoon. For this reason chai is sold just about everywhere. An expert at Chai.com, a Web site all about the beverage, explains: "Chai stalls are a favorite meeting place to savor a hot, fresh cup of chai and discuss the day's happenings. They are found all over India; from train stations in Bombay, to tiny villages around the country."[12]

Although it is made with black tea, chai tastes quite different from a simple cup of tea. To make chai, Indians boil water with a mix of spices known as chai masala. The spices include whole cardamom pods, cinnamon

Indian Ice Cream

Kulfi (kul-fee), which came from ancient Persia, is the Indian name for ice cream. Made with thickened and sweetened milk, kulfi is thicker and harder than Western ice cream but equally delicious. It is sold mainly in the summer, when vendors carry it door-to-door.

Kulfi comes in many flavors. Fruit and nut flavors are the most popular. Traditionally, kulfi was made by mixing milk, nuts, sugar, and sweet spices in a cone-shaped container. The container was sealed with dough, then placed in a clay tub filled with ice to freeze and harden. Cone-shaped kulfi containers are still used today. Modern Indians fill the containers with their favorite ingredients and then put them in their freezer to set.

Chai

Chai is easy to make. You can add more or less sugar or spices depending on your taste. A pinch of ginger can be substituted for cardamom or added to the mixture. A clove can also be added. Whole, low-fat, or nonfat milk can be used.

Ingredients

½ cup water
½ cinnamon stick
2 cardamom pods, crushed
1 cup milk
4 teaspoons sugar
2 teaspoons black tea or 2 tea bags

Instructions

1. Combine the water and spices in a sauce pan. Bring to a boil.
2. Add the milk and sugar to the pan. Over medium heat, bring the mixture to a boil.
3. Turn off the heat. Add the tea and cover the pot. Let the tea steep. The longer it steeps, the stronger and darker the tea will be.
4. Strain the mixture. Pour into a teapot and serve.

Serves 2.

sticks, peppercorns, and cloves. Once the mixture boils, tea, milk, and sugar are added. The sugar brings out the flavor of the spices. The mixture is boiled again, which causes the milk to get foamy, then left to simmer and steep. It is strained before it is served.

Chai is slightly thicker than plain tea, with a delightful milk froth. It tastes sweet and soothing and smells incredibly aromatic. Some people compare the scent to that of a hot pumpkin pie. In warm weather, ginger is often added. Indians say ginger cools the body. Extra cardamom, which is said to be warming, is added in winter.

Chai is usually served in a glass, and it is always piping hot. To cool it, drinkers pour the liquid back and forth from one glass to another. This also makes the drink foamy.

Indians love to get together with friends and drink chai, and they always offer a glass to guests. "Tea, as a beverage," notes Nupur, an Indian woman, "has been a way of life forever." In India, she explains, "tea is the beverage of choice."[13]

Street vendors tempt busy Indians with frothy spiced chai; crispy samosas, pakodas, pakoras, and panipuris; and juicy pav bhajis. Is it any wonder Indians love to snack? These tasty treats are hard to resist.

Chapter

Honored Guests

Hospitality is very important in India. "When a guest walks into your house," an Indian saying goes, "God comes with him."[14] That is why the finest food is reserved for guests.

A Unique Beverage

As soon as visitors enter an Indian home, they are offered a welcoming beverage. In southern India, **rasam** (rah-sahm) is specially prepared for this purpose. Rasam is similar to consommé. But instead of being made from beef or chicken broth, it is made from water flavored with sour fruits and savory spices. Indian cooks usually prepare a variety of rasams. This way guests can select their favorite.

Rasam is easy to make. Cooks combine the nutrient-rich water used to prepare legumes with lemon or tamarind juice. The latter is a tart tropical fruit. Hot black pepper and chili powder are added to the liquid, which is boiled and served in a glass. To sweeten the drink, pineapple juice, ginger, mint, or crushed tomatoes may be added.

Indians honor visiting friends and relatives by serving their favorite foods.

Jaggery

Most Indian sweets are made with unrefined sugar known as jaggery. It is a dark, coarse sugar that contains no chemicals or preservatives. Jaggery is made from sugar cane sap. The sap is boiled until it becomes syrup. The syrup hardens into coarse blocks.

Jaggery tastes like a blend of molasses and brown sugar. It contains vitamins, minerals, and protein and is said to have health benefits. In fact, it is used in Indian medicines to improve liver function and purify the blood.

Women gather to cook special dishes with jaggery during a religious festival.

Rasam is quite nutritious and is supposed to aid in digestion. It has a delicate flavor and a wonderful aroma. Ruth, who grew up in India, explains that rasam is "pleasantly light and spicy, delicately textured, but with sass."[15]

Layers of Rice

After a welcoming beverage, guests are always offered a wide array of foods. On special occasions, a rice and lamb casserole called **biriyani** (bi-ri-yaah-nee) is sure to be on the menu. It is also a popular dish among Indian Muslims during Ramadan. During that month-long holiday, many Indians fast during the day but feast in the evening with festive foods that almost always include biriyani.

Indians have been celebrating with biriyani for centuries. Historians think the dish was brought to India by the Moghuls (Mo-ghuls). These central Asians were

A Muslim vendor sells biriyani, a layered lamb and rice casserole, during Ramadan.

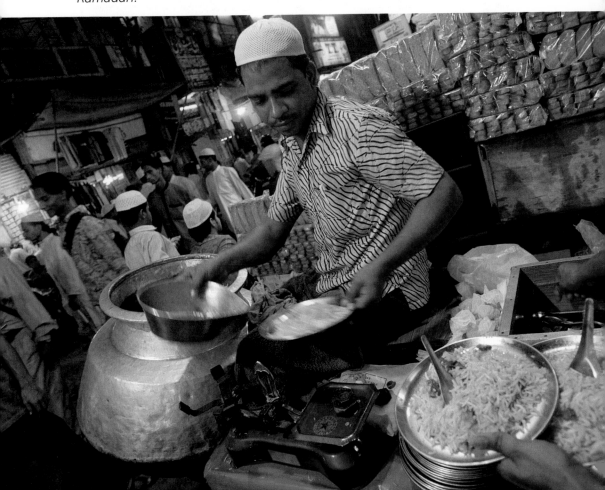

Biriyani (foreground) is a dish often served on special occasions.

descended from Genghis Khan. They ruled India from the 16th century until 1858.

To prepare biriyani, cooks make a spiced lamb stew like roghan josh or lamb korma. At the same time, they partially cook rice. The stew and rice are alternately layered one on top of the other. The dish is then covered and baked. As it bakes, the juice from the stew moistens, cooks, and flavors the rice. The end result is an edible work of art composed of brightly colored, contrasting layers, tantalizing fragrances, and a delicious blend of flavors. To add to the dish's appeal, Indian cooks often add fried onions, dried fruits, and nuts, and serve it with cucumber raita.

Because making biriyani is time-consuming, there are special biriyani makers who prepare made-to-order biriyani for busy Indians. Whether it is homemade or store bought, whenever biriyani is served, Indians know it is a special occasion.

It has been this way for centuries. According to chefs Smita and Sanjeev Chandra, in the 17th century, when the English ambassador was invited to dinner by the Moghul emperor, "[The] banquet centered on elaborate rice biriyanis, as was the custom in Moghul times." Modern banquets, they explain, "also give pride of place to biriyani."[16]

Fabulous Weddings

Biriyani is almost always served at Indian weddings. Among well-to-do families, weddings can be quite lavish. Some weddings involve hundreds of guests and

This Indian wedding ceremony will be followed by a lavish feast sure to include a large assortment of sweets.

many multiple-course banquets. Depending on the couple's religion, the menu may be vegetarian, or it may include lamb, meat, fish, and chicken dishes. Dozens of different spicy-sauced stews; a wide range of dals, chutneys, and raitas; tandoor-cooked specialties; rotis; and an array of rice and vegetables dishes may be served. But no matter what else is offered, there is always a large assortment of sweet desserts.

Mishani

When meat is served at Indian weddings, a two-day feast that consists of multiple lamb dishes known as a mishani (mi-shah-nee) is usually part of the menu. On the day of the wedding, the bride's family serves seven lamb dishes to welcome the guests. The next day the groom's family does the same, which means that fourteen different lamb dishes are served.

Lamb has always been popular in India, since it can be eaten by people of various religions. The tradition of serving multiple lamb courses at weddings began in ancient Persia and was brought to India by Persian traders. Popular mishani dishes include roghan josh, spiced lamb liver, lamb meatballs, shredded lamb cooked with yogurt and spices, lamb kebabs, roasted leg of lamb, and lamb kidneys.

A dish made with lamb will be served at an Indian wedding.

Lighting candles and sharing sweets are traditions of Diwali, the Hindu festival of lights.

Sweets have special meaning for most Indians. Hindus believe that honey, milk, sugar, and nuts are all gifts of the gods. Muslims say that nut- and fruit-filled sweets are symbols of wealth and bring good luck to all who eat them. For both groups, offering sweets to wedding guests is a way to show love and friendship. And **laapsi** (lahp-see), a hot, porridge-like dish, is one of the most popular, especially among Hindus.

Laapsi is made of cracked wheat, sugar, and water. The wheat is slowly fried in ghee until it turns a deep, dark red. Then water is spilled over the grain, and the mixture is cooked until it is dry and soft. Before it is served, syrup made from sugar and water is poured over the top. It is then decorated with slivered almonds.

Laapsi has a sweet nutty taste and a soft, comforting texture. Unlike the rest of the desserts, which are usually served by waiters or buffet-style, the bride and groom themselves almost always serve laapsi to their guests. This is a way for the wedding couple to show respect to their guests and thank them for joining in the celebration.

Sharing Sweets

Sweets are also shared during festivals and holidays. For example, giving sweets to visitors is an important part of **Diwali** (Dee-wah-lee), the five-day Hindu festival of lights. Diwali is a happy occasion marked by fireworks, brightly lit lanterns, and sweet treats.

Many of these treats feature coconut, which Hindu myths say is a favorite food of the gods. Sharing coconut treats with guests lets them know that they are held

Coconut

in the highest esteem. Baljekar notes: "The very sight of coconut conjures up images of religious occasions in India. . . . For every religious event coconut is placed in a prominent place on a full pot of rice." Its presence, she explains, symbolizes "a life full of rich experiences."[17]

Coconut Barfi

Barfi is made like fudge and hardens to a similar texture. It is not difficult to make. You can decorate each piece with a sliver of almond or a cashew nut.

Ingredients
1 cup milk
½ cup butter
2 cups grated coconut
2 cups sugar

Instructions
1. Combine milk and butter in a saucepan and bring to a boil.
2. Lower the heat. Stir in the coconut and sugar. Cook until the mixture thickens enough to roll it into a ball in your hand, about five to ten minutes.
3. Grease a shallow pan with butter or nonstick spray. Remove the coconut mix from the heat and pour it into the pan, spreading it thinly. Allow it to cool.
4. Cut into twelve squares. Store the barfi in an airtight container.

Serves 12.

On special occasions, Indians serve sweet treats wrapped in silver foil.

For this reason, and because it is delicious, coconut **barfi** (bar-fee) is likely to be served. This fudgelike sweet is made by heating together grated coconut, sugar, and milk or water. The hot mixture is poured into a pan and left to harden. Then it is cut into little squares or diamonds. To make the treat really special, each piece may be adorned with or wrapped in an edible silver leaf. This decoration, which has no taste, has been used in India for centuries. It adds beauty to desserts served during

Diwali Rice Pudding

Special rice pudding is always served on the final night of Diwali. It is not hard to make but does take time.

Ingredients
4 cups milk
½ cup long-grain rice
1 cup sugar
½ cup raisins
1 teaspoon ground cardamom
½ cup almonds, chopped

Instructions
1. Pour the milk into a large saucepan and bring to a boil.
2. Add the rice. Lower the heat and cook slowly until the rice is cooked and the mixture is creamy, about one hour. Stir frequently so the rice does not stick to the pan.
3. When the rice is done, add the sugar, raisins, cardamom, and almonds. Stir well. The pudding can be served hot or it can be chilled and served cold.

Serves 4.

special occasions. Silver leaf is made from small balls of sterling silver. These are placed in leather pouches, where they are hammered down into powder, flakes, or tissue-thin sheets. "Lots of Indian sweets have an edible silver leaf coating," explains Sukanya, who grew up in India. "It is used to add a special final touch."[18]

The silver leaf is also used to decorate and wrap other holiday treats such as cashew or pistachio barfi. It is often sprinkled on **kheer** (keer), a fragrant and creamy rice pudding flavored with dried fruit and nuts. It is almost always served on the last night of Diwali. And it is often used as a wrapping for coconut ladoos (lah-doos). These are small, ball-shaped sweets made with grated coconut, sugar, condensed milk and decorated with almonds, pistachios, or sesame seeds. Indians say that eating these treats sweetens the diner's personality. Eat them, an old saying goes, "and speak sweet words."[19]

Diners cannot help but speak sweet words when they are served special foods like coconut barfi, kheer, ladoos, biriyani, and rasam. These treats help make guests feel special and make every occasion memorable.

Metric Conversions

Mass (weight)

1 ounce (oz.)	= 28.0 grams (g)
8 ounces	= 227.0 grams
1 pound (lb.) or 16 ounces	= 0.45 kilograms (kg)
2.2 pounds	= 1.0 kilogram

Liquid Volume

1 teaspoon (tsp.)	= 5.0 milliliters (ml)
1 tablespoon (tbsp.)	= 15.0 milliliters
1 fluid ounce (oz.)	= 30.0 milliliters
1 cup (c.)	= 240 milliliters
1 pint (pt.)	= 480 milliliters
1 quart (qt.)	= 0.96 liters (l)
1 gallon (gal.)	= 3.84 liters

Pan Sizes

8-inch cake pan	= 20 x 4-centimeter cake pan
9-inch cake pan	= 23 x 3.5-centimeter cake pan
11 x 7-inch baking pan	= 28 x 18-centimeter baking pan
13 x 9-inch baking pan	= 32.5 x 23-centimeter baking pan
9 x 5-inch loaf pan	= 23 x 13-centimeter loaf pan
2-quart casserole	= 2-liter casserole

Length

1/4 inch (in.)	= 0.6 centimeters (cm)
1/2 inch	= 1.25 centimeters
1 inch	= 2.5 centimeters

Temperature

212° F	= 100° C (boiling point of water)
225° F	= 110° C
250° F	= 120° C
275° F	= 135° C
300° F	= 150° C
325° F	= 160° C
350° F	= 180° C
375° F	= 190° C
400° F	= 200° C

Notes

Chapter 1: Colorful, Fragrant, and Delicious

1. Mridula Baljekar, *Secrets from an Indian Kitchen*. London: Pavilion Books, 2000, p. 12.

2. Martin Hughes, Sheema Mookherjee, and Richard Delacy, *World Food India*. Victoria, Australia: Lonely Planet, 2001, p. 49.

3. Indian Foods Company, "Flat Breads," www.indianfoods co.com/ Recipes/breads.htm.

4. Suvir Saran and Stephanie Lyness, *Indian Home Cooking*. New York: Clarkson Potter, 2004, p. 30.

Chapter 2: Common Threads

5. Saran and Lyness, *Indian Home Cooking*, p. 110.

6. Baljekar, *Secrets from an Indian Kitchen*, p. 78.

7. Golden Tandoors, "Clay Ovens," www.goldentandoors.com/ products/clay-ovens.htm.

8. Diane Seed, *Favorite Indian Food*. Berkeley, CA: Ten Speed, 1990, p. 114.

Chapter 3: Tasty Snacks

9. Hughes, Mookherjee, and Delacy, *World Food India*, p. 232.

10. Baljekar, *Secrets from an Indian Kitchen*, p. 106.

11. Gel's Kitchen, "Pav Bhaji," www.gelskitchen.com/view/recipes/ rec/10019/-/.

12. Chai.com, "What Is Chai?" http://chai.com/chai.html.

13. Quoted in One Hot Stove, "IMBB17: A Taste Tea Obsession," http://one hotstove.blogspot.com/2005/07/imbb17-taste tea-obsession. html.

Chapter 4: Honored Guests
14. Saran and Lyness, *Indian Home Cooking*, p. 9.

15. Quoted in Soup Song, "Rasam," www.soupsong.com/rrasam. html.

16. Smita Chandra and Sanjeev Chandra, *Cuisines of India.* New York: Ecco Press; HarperCollins, 2001, p. 132.

17. Baljekar, *Secrets from an Indian Kitchen*, p. 94.

18. Sukanya, e-mail interview with the author, April 24, 2006.

19. Hughes, Mookherjee, and Delacy, *World Food India*, p. 303.

Glossary

barfi: A fudgelike sweet.

biriyani: A layered rice casserole.

chaats: Snack foods, which are usually deep-fried.

chai: Sweet, milky, spiced tea.

chapati: A type of Indian flat bread.

chutneys: Relishes made with fresh fruits and vegetables and spices.

dal: A stewlike dish made with legumes and spices.

Diwali: The Hindu festival of lights.

garam masala: A blend of up to fifteen ground spices widely used in Indian cooking.

ghee: Butter in which all the milk solids have been removed.

kari: An herb commonly used to spice sauces.

kheer: A popular rice pudding.

kormas: Sweet and mild, stewlike dishes.

laapsi: A sweet, porridge-like dish, which is often served at weddings.

masala: Any combination of ground spices.

naan: A flat bread made in a tandoor.

paranthas: Pastry-like flat breads.

pav bhaji: A bread-and-vegetable mixture eaten as a snack.

pooris: Deep-fried flat breads.

raitas: Relishes that blend yogurt with raw vegetables or fruit and spices.

rasam: A soup similar to consommé.

roghan josh: A spicy stew usually made with lamb.

rotis: Flat breads.

tandoor: A clay oven.

tawa: A hot, cast-iron griddle used to cook flat breads.

vindaloo: A spicy, sweet-and-sour, sauced dish.

For Further Exploration

Books

Arlette N. Braman, *Kids Around the World Cook! The Best Foods and Recipes from Many Lands*. New York: John Wiley & Sons, 2000. This international kid's cookbook includes a recipe from India.

Melanie Guile, *Culture in India*. Chicago: Raintree, 2005. A colorful book with lots of pictures that looks at India's holidays, daily life, history, and people.

Bobbie Kalman, *India: The Culture*. New York: Crabtree, 2000. This book explores Indian art, music, foods, and festivals.

Matthew Locricchio, *The Cooking of India*. New York: Benchmark, 2004. This is Indian recipe book for kids.

Vijay Madavan, *Cooking the Indian Way*. Minneapolis: Lerner, 2002. This is a simple Indian recipe book for children.

Web Sites

History For Kids, "Ancient India," (www.historyforkids. org/learn/india/). This site offers lots of information about life in ancient India and includes a discussion of foods, a timeline, and craft activities.

Indian Food Forever (www.indianfoodforever.com). This Web site for adults has lots of recipes, including microwave recipes. It also has a glossary.

Ruchis Kitchen (www.ruchiskitchen.com). Adults and kids can find lots of recipes, information about dozens of Indian holidays and festivals, and fictional children's stories set in India on this site.

Snaith Primary School, "Welcome to India" (http://home. freeuk.net/elloughton13/india.htm). Maintained by a British elementary school, this Web site has lots of information about India prepared just for kids. It includes pictures, stories, and facts about life in India.

Time for Kids, "Go Places India" (www.timeforkids. com/TFK/specials/goplaces/0,12405,214513,00.html). This colorful Web site provides a sightseeing guide with lots of pictures, historical information, stories, audio phrases in Hindi, and information about current problems in India.

Index

Picture credits

About the Author

Barbara Sheen is the author of numerous books for young people. She lives in New Mexico with her family. In her spare time, she likes to swim, walk, garden, and read. And, of course, she loves to cook!